CHRISTIANITY

AND

PLURALISM

T0311361

CHRISTIANITY

AND

PLURALISM

RON DART & J. I. PACKER

LEXHAM PRESS

Christianity and Pluralism

Lexham Press, 1313 Commercial St., Bellingham, WA 98225
LexhamPress.com

Originally published as *In a Pluralist World* by Regent College
Publishing (1998).

Print ISBN 9781683592877
Digital ISBN 9781683592884

Lexham Editorial Team: Todd Hains, Danielle Thevenaz
Cover Design: Peter Park
Typesetting: Scribe Inc.

CONTENTS

PREFACE TO
THE NEW EDITION

It's a perennial dialogue: how do the various religions inter-relate? Was Jesus merely a Jewish rabbi, a forerunner of Muhammad, a Hindu avatar, a Buddhist bodhisattva, a crypto-gnostic, or a Sufi in disguise? Or are Judaism, Christianity, Islam, Taoism, Hinduism, Buddhism, and other religious tra-ditions all diverse paths to a similar goal? These questions tend to dominate interfaith dialogue.

The publication in 1997 of Bishop Michael Ingham's *Mansions of the Spirit: The Gospel in a Multi-Faith World* brought such ques-tions to the fore once again. Bishop Ingham was, at the time, the Anglican Bishop of the diocese in New Westminster (British Columbia), and his challenging missive could not be ignored. Ingham pondered four models as a way of answering the multi-faith issue: inclusivist, exclusivist, pluralist, and a form of subtle syncretism. He advocated subtle syncretism in which mystics of most religions were in agreement in a hidden way.

This extreme form of ideological liberalism—as also embod-ied in the life and work of John Hick and Bishops Ingham, John Spong, William Swing, and Richard Holloway (to name a few)—alerted conservatives to a more serious problem in the life of the church: the subversion of Christian truth claims. *Mansions of the Spirit* required a response that was neither uncritical nor excessively critical—a thoughtful and reasoned third way of sorts.

And so this short book was commissioned by a group of conservative Anglicans in the Anglican Church of Canada, who brought together a more classical catholic form of Anglicanism with Reformed, evangelical, and charismatic tendencies. (They were known as the Essentials Group; they convened the Essentials Conference in Montreal in 1995.[1]) Regent College (Vancouver, BC) originally published this as *In a Pluralist World*, part of the Charting Our Course series in 1998.

Mansions of the Spirit was, in many ways, a popular rendition of the Primordial Tradition. The Primordial Tradition takes the position that religions are separate and discrete ways to God, the Ultimate, the Infinite (various names used), and yet they cannot and should not be synthesized—each of these traditions offer legitimate ways, when followed in a disciplined and faithful path, to the higher esoteric and mystical heights of a greater unity. It is the mystics within each of the traditions that reveal this hidden unity in contrast to external diversity.

However, mystics do not all agree on the nature of union with the Ultimate. The Primordial Tradition tends to skew the facts and choose selective mystics that fit its predetermined thesis. In fact, the mystics of various traditions diverge greatly in their approaches to and understanding of God—if they even believe in a god—and their understanding of the ultimate purpose of humanity.

The actual historic reason and context for *Mansions of the Spirit* and *In a Pluralist World* are—except for those who lived through such a moment of history—mostly forgotten. But the

---

1. The proceedings were published as *Anglican Essentials: Reclaiming Faith Within the Anglican Church of Canada*, ed. George Egerton (Toronto: Anglican Book Centre, 1995).

same questions remain. We need to ask substantive questions about our society's pluralistic approach to a variety of issues, including our multi-faith world. It is not very liberal of a liberal not to critique liberalism. But many liberals seem unable to question their blindspots—such is the nature of ideology. They signal openness to the legitimate nature of alternate readings of timely and timeless issues, yet they are actually quite closed to such.

Many today continue to assume that history moves in an upward and positive direction—those bygone eras weren't quite as enlightened as we are.

Hermann Hesse offers a nuanced and subtle critique of such people in his Nobel Prize winning novel, *The Glass Bead Game.* At its core *The Glass Bead Game* is about elite and highly educated contemplative intellectuals who weave together varied beads of thought—the best that had been thought, said, and done across time and cultures—into a grand and unified vision. It was assumed that this metanarrative of spiritual unity would bring an end to wars, poverty, and division. The many cultures, civilizations, tribes, and clans that had fought and destroyed one another again and again throughout history would now be united.

And that's the hope of many intellectuals today.

But Hesse had witnessed the betrayal of the loftiest ideals during World War I and World War II. *The Glass Bead Game* makes it abundantly clear that the naïve idealism of a universal synthesis will often be betrayed and subverted by power politics, nationalism, and tribal interests—the unfortunate realities of our fallen world that the synthesis is meant to overcome.

Pluralism and syncretism can be as exclusivist as any of the positions they rail against as being exclusive.

Ron Dart
University of the Fraser Valley
January 2019

PREFACE

In the autumn of 1997, Bishop Michael Ingham reopened a long-standing debate within the Anglican Church of Canada (and within most other denominations as well) by the publication of his book, *Mansions of the Spirit: The Gospel in a Multi-Faith World*. The central topic is the validity of the Christian gospel concerning the uniqueness of Jesus Christ in a religiously pluralistic world. But, as Michael himself acknowledges in his book, this issue is inextricably intertwined with other matters such as the authority of Scripture and the place of evangelism in the church at the beginning of the twenty-first century. This booklet contains some early responses to *Mansions of the Spirit* from two members, one lay and one ordained, of the bishop's own diocese of New Westminster.

Mr. Ron Dart is a highly respected academic trained in the study of world religion who was a founder of the department of world religions at the University College of the Fraser Valley. Ron's two contributions here speak to the different ways in which inter-faith encounters can be approached, and he dispassionately outlines the strengths and weaknesses of each. His articles suggest that ultimately *Mansions of the Spirit* (particularly in the last three chapters) moves in the direction of a modified syncretist approach to inter-faith relations.

The Reverend Dr. J. I. Packer is a widely published theologian at Regent College with an international reputation. Jim's paper in this booklet is both pastoral and theological and is particularly helpful in addressing the dilemma of how a Christian can hold to the New Testament truth without sacrificing care for those outside the Christian tradition, a dilemma which *Mansions of the Spirit* fails to resolve.

I commend these papers to your prayerful reading and reflection. May they help each of us discern the core issues in this debate. Then may we openly and honestly discuss the issues with an integrity that transcends name-calling ("fundamentalist" and "heretic," for example). Our church can only be strengthened by a spirited yet irenic grappling with Truth.

The Reverend Dr. Archie Pell
Christ Church, Hope, B.C.
The Feast of the Conversion of St. Paul, 1998

CHAPTER 1

CHRISTIANITY OR RELIGIOUS PLURALISM?

A Review of *Mansions of the Spirit*

Ron Dart

I call for a pluralism that allows each religious tradition to define its own nature and purposes and the role of religious elements within it.

—J. Cobb

The fact that we live in a global village means that we inhabit a world in which people of various faith communities mix and mingle. The "splendid isolation" (if it ever did exist) of the past few centuries has come to a close. This means that all the major and minor religions of the world (and all sorts of new ones) are faced with making sense of their truth claims in a multi-faith context. The appeal of Michael Ingham's *Mansions of the Spirit* is the way he is keen and eager to face the hard questions of our ethos and not flinch from offering some difficult and challenging paths to hike. *Mansions of the Spirit* opens the reader to some new vistas that must be seen and sensitively responded to. Michael acknowledges that we live in a multi-faith and pluralistic context; who would deny such a reality? The response to this reality has come from a diversity of directions. The inter-faith movement, beginning with the Parliament of World's Religions in 1893 and culminating with the successful 1993 Parliament, is discussed in some detail; many other inter-faith groups are, also, mentioned in passing. The multi-faith movement is a response to the obvious reality of religious pluralism, and it is a movement that Michael has some sympathy and interest in.

A significant segment of *Mansions of the Spirit* examines four models for inter-faith dialogue. The first three models (exclusive, inclusive, pluralist) are explored and explained, and the validity and limitation of each is discussed. It is difficult to know how Michael finally evaluates the fourth model (transcendent syncretism of the Primordial tradition), but this will be discussed later.

I think the church should welcome *Mansions of the Spirit*; it has forced the people of God to think more deeply and clearly about what they believe and why. There can be no shrinking from the fact that religious pluralism opens us up to some rather significant questions for the Christian community, and *Mansions of the Spirit* is one way of solving some of the pressing issues. I find, though, I must beg to differ with Michael's position, and the trail he would have us trek. There are ten points I will, all too briefly, raise in this review; hopefully, these questions will nudge the issues raised in *Mansions of the Spirit* to a deeper level and enrich the meaning of dialogue.

First, Michael seems to think that we, as Western Christians in the latter half of the twentieth century, are facing "a new phenomenon." The modern fact of pluralism, though, for the West is not new. In fact, Christianity was birthed and matured in the classical and late antique world; the Roman culture of the time was thick with pluralism and syncretism. The New Testament, postapostolic, and patristic writers swam in the waters of immense religious diversity and had to make sense of their faith within such a religious and philosophical context. The church, as it moved north from its early Mediterranean setting, constantly faced new and different cultures and religions. The period of European expansion that followed the Reformation meant that Christianity was once again exposed to other faith traditions. So, rather than assuming we live on the cusp of a new moment of history, it is much wiser to realize we have been here many times before. Déjà vu rather than chronological snobbery should be a more appropriate stance. In short, there are serious reasons for calling into question that this is a "new phenomenon" or "new context."

Second, Michael is quick to highlight the strengths and limitations of the exclusive model. He, rightly so, points out how the exclusive approach can be used and has been used to justify some of the worst forms of cultural oppression. I don't think many would disagree with Michael on this telling point. Michael further argues that the exclusivists tend to lack a certain sense of the historical nature of biblical texts and means to interpret them. Again, this might be true of some exclusivists. Michael, then, argues that the Council of Florence, the Lausanne Declaration, the Congress on World Mission, and the Essentials movement stand within the exclusive tribe; there is no doubt there is much truth in this, and the differences between these groups is ably and nimbly discussed by Michael. The fact that exclusivism can be found in other religious traditions is, also, acknowledged by *Mansions of the Spirit.* I can't help but feeling, though, that Michael has caricatured exclusivism by presenting some of its worst faces. There is a sophisticated form of exclusivism that Michael has ignored. A good dose of Barth would have helped.

Third, Michael turns to the Primordial tradition of Schuon and Smith (with their notion of the transcendent unity of religions) as a reply to the failures of the exclusive, inclusive, and pluralist models, but it is difficult for the reader to know whether he accepts the lead of the Primordial tradition or whether its distinction between esoterics (mystics with the true insight) and exoterics (those who live within a historic tradition) must be scorned when day is done. There is little doubt that mystics, from various religious traditions, do not agree about the nature of the Ultimate, as much as the gurus of the Primordial tradition would like us to think. G. Parrinder's *Mysticism in the World's Religions* gives the lie to this perennial notion. So, if the "mystical path" in Eckhart, Mechtild, and Merton are suggestive but not definitive of a common essence, where are we then? Since the exclusive, inclusive, and pluralist models have their Achilles' heels and blind spots, where do we go for insight?

Fourth, Michael, rightly so, is quick to point out that higher and lower criticism are crucial for any sane understanding of how to approach the Bible; most of the thoughtful would agree with this. The problem comes, though, when we begin the task of sorting through what are the words of Jesus and what are the words of the church. Michael tends to be rather hard on the exclusivists when they seem to ignore these issues, but the danger, of course, is that each clan picks the texts that suits their agenda and ignores or rationalizes away what doesn't. History is replete with the game of textual Russian Roulette. The texts we chose to elevate often say more about our leanings than anything else. Surely Gadamer's "Truth and Method," critical theory, and the school of hermeneutical suspicion teach us as much.

Fifth, Michael, in various places, makes a distinction between theology (that has its limits) and mysticism that can give us clearer and cleaner insight. I find this distinction somewhat forced and rather artificial. As soon as the mystics or contemplatives speak (or don't), theology is being done. It is much more honest to state that mystics are theologians and good theologians are mystics. The issue should not be between mystic and theologian, but what is the content or insight offered by the mystical theologian? The distinction Michael has made, of course, plays into the exoteric-theologian/esoteric-mystic approach, but I would suggest that such an either-or distinction is more reacting to a bad form of theology. Mystical theologians do differ on their view of the Ultimate; hence the issue is not so much opposing mystic and theologian as weighing what is communicated.

Sixth, Michael, in "Drawing the Circle Wider," seems to be suggesting that there is this upward, evolutionary, and developmental process going on in the Bible and religious thinking. This sort of Hegelian dialectic can be refuted from the stubborn facts of history. The Bible has parochial-nationalist tendencies and more inclusivist leanings. It is not that one emerges and evolves from the other, though. The polyphonic nature of the Bible (and Western history and intellectual thought for that matter) highlights how many voices are often speaking at the same time; hence history can be seen more as a contest (*agon*) between varied and competing positions. We do not need to read the text as some incremental and upward arc into a sort of syncretistic or pluralist perspective. I think it can be argued that exclusivism, inclusivism, pluralism, and varieties of syncretism have been at work at the same time throughout history. The Christian tradition, at its best, has been a blend of prophetic exclusivism and enlightened inclusivism, and these models have an ancient lineage.

Seventh, it is difficult to sort out where Michael finally is willing to plant his flag. He makes it clear that the exclusive, inclusive, and pluralist models won't work. He seems to be pointing in chapters 8–10 to a sort of transcendent unity. If the mystical path, grounded openness, and drawing the circle wider mean anything, they seem to have something to do with pluralism (which Michael sees the difficulties with) and a sort of transcendent syncretism. The final chapters of *Mansions of the Spirit*, then, have a sort of unresolved tension and ambiguity about them. Is Michael, when day is done, genuflecting before the Primordial tradition? If not, is he doffing his cap to pluralism? Kung, Pannenberg, and Newbigin have surely warned him about the pitfalls of either a crude pluralism or a sophisticated pluralism. A sort of unresolved critical pluralism and transcendent syncretism leave the reader with a sense that this book needs more thought, and the author needs to get off the fence.

Eighth, Michael, in his discussion of the mystics, highlights how most of the mystics and good theologians talk about a "God beyond God" or "Wordless Godhead" or "Nameless Nothing" and many other names that suggest and point to the grand mystery of God. The Christian tradition has, of course, this approach; we call it the *apophatic* or negative way. The essence of such an approach is that no concept or image can exhaust the Divine; we, also, have the *cataphatic* and positive way. This is where the real dialogue begins. God is thick with mystery, and many of the mystics long for some sort of *unio mystica* with the Divine. The issue, though, is this: there are many intermediate forms between the Divine and the human; there are many mediums (gurus, sages, avatars, bodhisattvas) between God and humankind. Are they all equal and merely appropriate for different times and places, or is Christ, in fact, the fullness of the Godhead bodily? It would certainly be helpful if Michael had come much cleaner on this issue; the Christian tradition has in its long encounter and multiple contacts with other religions.

Ninth, I wonder why Michael has chosen the mystical path as his model for inter-faith dialogue; he could have chosen the prophetic or wisdom traditions or some sort of subtle blend of all three. I would think a blend of all three approaches rather than the mystical would have borne fuller fruit. It would have been interesting to see how a solid and radical prophetic approach would have taken *Mansions of the Spirit* in a different direction. Michael, for the most part, ends up with a rather predictable tract on a sort of mystical social liberalism; such a conclusion is very much a child of the humanistic wing of the Enlightenment.

Tenth, *Mansions of the Spirit* would have been much stronger if a solid and serious comparison/contrast between religious founders, texts, commentaries, or communities had been done. It is hard to know where Michael views Christianity in the world of major and minor religions. Is Jesus "God made man" so that all humanity can be lifted up and deified, or is Jesus a light of the Divine? If the former, then *Mansions of the Spirit* should state this and develop this argument in a fuller manner. If not, then Jesus as a son of God is merely on par with other avatars and bodhisattvas. Again, as in much of *Mansions of the Spirit* some clarity is called for rather than fence sitting.

In conclusion, I find that the three appendixes in *Mansions of the Spirit* clearly place this timely text within the

Enlightenment-liberal establishment tradition; those who live, move, and have their being within this tradition will welcome, quite uncritically, the insights of *Mansions of the Spirit*. Those, though, who find the *Statements of the Lambeth Conference on Other Religions*, Küng's *Towards a Global Ethic*, and *Guidelines for Inter-Faith Dialogue of the Anglican Church of Canada* as needing some healthy and robust criticism will long for something more substantive. As someone who has been taught and nurtured by the radical Anglo-Catholics, I find that *Mansions of the Spirit* lacks a rigorous mystical theology, a radical politics, and a high Christology-ecclesiology. I think, without such a full vision of what Christianity has been, is, and ever shall be, inter-faith dialogue will lack a certain depth and challenging honesty.

CHAPTER 2

THE WAY, THE TRUTH, AND THE LIFE

A Discussion of *Mansions of the Spirit*

J. I. Packer

Michael Ingham, Bishop of New Westminster, is a nice man. We who form his diocese knew that before; now *Mansions of the Spirit* makes it plain to every reader.

Throughout this book, Bishop Michael comes across as a person of great goodwill who loves peace, who hates bigotry and violence of every kind, who abhors the fierce dogmatism that sets people at each other's throats and the proud elitism that says some people do not matter, and who wants to see religion operating as a force for world peace rather than world war. To this end he aims to affirm all the world's main religions and all those who practice them, and wants to see religion spread among the many whose very humanity is at risk for their current lack of it.

To be sure, there is one form of religion that is clearly anathema to him. He ascribes this repugnant form to what he calls "the conservative-evangelical-fundamentalist coalition" but which two millennia of history entitle us to describe as mainstream Christianity. This is the view that Jesus Christ is the second person of the Trinity incarnate, that personal discipleship to him is the only path of eternal life, and that making disciples of all the nations is the church's unending primary task. Roman Catholicism, Eastern Orthodoxy, and classical Protestantism share at least a nominal commitment to this belief, which world Anglicanism also shared till about fifty years ago. Bishop Michael does not understand it well and is unable to be fully respectful and temperate in what he says about it. But otherwise he is charmingly sympathetic and courteous to a fault toward all the positions of which he takes notice.

The sad burden of the present critique is that Bishop Michael's niceness and passion to affirm people has led him to a position that in effect abolishes what Anglicans generally, indeed Christians generally, understand Christianity to be. Yet the niceness itself is a quality to appreciate, and the proper way to start is surely by celebrating the fact that Michael displays it so fully.

What, now, of his book? First let us note that its title, *Mansions of the Spirit*, is a phrase lifted from Robert Runcie, former Archbishop of Canterbury, who in a public lecture in 1993 declared that "dialogue can help us recognize that other faiths than our own are genuine mansions of the Spirit with many rooms to be discovered.... From the perspective of *faith*, different world religions can be seen as different gifts of the Spirit to humanity" (cited, p. 33). This in essence is the precise persuasion that Bishop Michael wants to share with us. It is significant that Michael sought an endorsement of his book both from Runcie himself and also from the Dalai Lama of Tibet; it is doubly significant that the Dalai Lama gave him one. Michael wishes to turn the Christian world mission into worldwide inter-faith dialogue in which no one changes their faith but all are enriched by coming to understand the faiths of others. The Dalai Lama's comment expressed his approval of this.

Is Michael's agenda new? Some readers will find it novel, particularly as coming from a bishop, but as Michael explains it has always been the program of the inter-faith movement that broke the surface with the 1893 Parliament of the World's Religions, and it has in fact been advocated from different quarters in the world of liberal Protestant thought since the 1920s at least. As Bishop Michael said in a newspaper interview at the time of his book's release, there is little here that is new to Christian scholars: "All I have tried to do is crystallize a lot of academic work into readable form."

The book has a subtitle, "The Gospel in a Multi-Faith World." We should now note that both title, and subtitle, illustrate one of the strategies of which those in what Michael calls "the modernist-liberal-progressive coalition" constantly avail themselves, namely using historic Christian terms, drawn from the Bible, in an altered sense. This habit, though perhaps inevitable, creates problems. It encourages the users to feel closer to the authentic Christian heritage than they really are, and not to see how far they have moved away from it. The hearers take the words as meaning what they themselves mean by them, so that the communication is deceptive in its effect. Ambiguity, double-talk, fuzzy speech, and fuzzy thought become unavoidable, and understanding is blocked. Michael's title and subtitle already reflect this.

"Spirit" in the title is not being used in the historic Trinitarian sense (indeed, on the showing of this book, Bishop Michael is not a historic Trinitarian at all). Michael understands the word as an evocative yet uninformative image for what Runcie called "the Divine" and what he himself is happy to call "the Nameless Nothing, which is at the heart of everything" (p. 111). And "Gospel" in the subtitle is not being used in the historic apostolic sense, in which it signifies non-negotiable truths about judgment, Jesus, and joy that constitute the good news from God. At one point Michael states, "What I am arguing for is a commitment among Christians to a gospel that compels us beyond fundamentalism to see in other religions the God we know in Jesus Christ" (p. 138). Whatever exactly this implies, it is clearly on a different wavelength from that of all the New Testament writers.

What is Michael's wavelength? It is an evolutionary hypothesis about world religion and world welfare, as we have already begun to see. The idea is that as the Old Testament chronicles an "emerging God-consciousness" (p. 128) that turned Yahweh from a local deity, one of many, into the God of the whole earth, and as the Jesus-event enlarged that God-consciousness ("the religious imagination," p. 132) into an affirmation of God's love for all, so the religious pluralism of our latter-day global village should enlarge our God-consciousness still further, to find in other faiths the same grace that Christians know. Michael's handling, or mishandling, of Scripture, his down slapping of the positions he calls exclusivism, inclusivism, and pluralism, and his zealous exposition of "grounded openness" on the basis of the theorizing in Frithjof Schuon's *The Transcendent Unity of Religions* (1993), put out by the Theosophical Publishing House, is all special pleading for this hypothesis. The bishop's book is cleverly calculated advocacy all the way. This must be borne in mind as we proceed.

To pull the threads together, then: Why did Bishop Michael write his book? For two reasons, it seems.

First reason: to promote inter-faith dialogue, with ground rules that are egalitarian (all world religions are ways to God and deserve equal honor) and trans-theological (no world religion offers definitive conceptual truth in its dogmas, though all make contact with "the Truth that transcends the truth," p. 123). Such dialogue, Michael believes, would lead to healthy recognition of defects in all religious traditions, and would promote religious peace world-wide and religious enrichment all round.

Second reason: to be honest in letting the church know what he stands for, and in coming clean about some of his purposes in his own diocese. Bishop Michael has the courage of his convictions; whatever we think of his views, we must admire him as a gutsy man who takes the risk of putting his cards on the table. Michael's honesty sets a searching standard for responses (this one, for instance).

Whom should we see him as addressing most directly? The book is brief (less than 140 pages by Michael himself); it is non-technical (there are no footnotes, page references, or index, and only a short one-sided bibliography "for the interested general reader"); and it is written in a sort of pulpitese which, though smooth-flowing and clear on the surface, is sometimes logically loose. Michael's ideal reader seems to be a middlebrow layperson, Anglican or Anglican-like, for whom religion, meaning observances (public worship and private prayer), lifestyle (uprightness and friendliness), and social concern (poverty and the environment), has importance, but who does not care about theology, or the difference between one faith and another. A hostile critic might say that Michael writes for Anglicans who are half-way to Hinduism in order in effect to take them right there; a fairer statement might be that he sees their sort of Anglicanism as basically right, so he gives them a theology to support it while rousing their interest in multi-faith conversations and witness to Jesus Christ in the course of them. But the book in fact challenges everyone who has any sense of historic Anglican identity, and it must be dealt with accordingly.

THE STORY LINE

Mansions unfolds thus. After relating how an experience in India showed him that his lack of interest in Hinduism was wrong, and urging that neighbor-love in the religiously plural-ist and spiritually impoverished West requires active involve-ment with others' religions (chapters 1 and 2), Bishop Michael tracks the inter-faith movement since 1893 (chapter 3), and generalizes about it as follows:

> Both within the religions themselves, as well as among those who have abandoned traditional orthodoxies altogether, there is a desire for mutual cooperation and practical action to replace missionary competition. And there is also a new search for a global theology— not to replace the different religions but to compre-hend them with a unifying vision. (p. 47)

To serve the inter-faith movement by providing such a the-ology is, as we have seen, Bishop Michael's goal. We pause here to clarify what is happening. Definitions first. By "religion" Michael means any and every professed recognition of a reality, or order of reality, that links present and future welfare with a stated way of life. The reality may be one God, or many gods, or the retributive, reincarnation principle that Hinduism calls *karma*, or the alluring prospect of the enlightenment which Buddhism calls *nirvana*, or maybe something else; but religion is viewed throughout as a generic human phenomenon, of which each particular religion is a species. Then "theology" means a religion's account of itself from within, and a "global" theology means an account from within religion as a universal human fact, involving the adherents of all particular religions in brotherly embrace. That is what Michael is after, as we said.

But "the claim to truth lies at the heart of each religion's self-understanding" (p. 50), and these claims clash. "If it is true, for example, that Jesus is the Messiah, the one predicted in the Hebrew Scriptures, how can it also be true—as Jews still believe—that the Messiah is yet to come? Or again, if it is true, as Muslims believe, that the Qur'an replaces and supersedes the revelations given through Moses and Jesus, how can it also be true, in the words of the Bhagavad Gita, that 'I am in every religion as the thread through a string of pearls'? The fact is, the world's religious doctrines are often mutually contradictory" (p. 50). "Theology by itself can never bring about agreement on the question of truth" (p. 51).

So what to do? Here the ways divide.

Historic Christianity, appealing to God's revelation in Jesus Christ and in the Bible, as the church has always done, diagnoses non-Christian religions as more or less mistaken and inadequate; maintains this stance under secular pressure from outside and revisionist pressure from inside; and seeks to share the knowledge of Christ in a converting way with everyone.

Bishop Michael presents an alternative program, as follows: On the one hand, appealing as liberals do to the generic reality of religion as such, and pointing to the multi-faith mix in countries like Canada, he declines to give Christianity pride of place, or any corrective role, in relation to non-Christian religions. And whereas historic Christianity sees adherence to the negative biblical judgment on non-Christian faiths as humble faithfulness to God, Michael views it as expressing a proud claim to be "superior" and as an imperialism that makes the all-on-a-level dialogue he favors impossible, so naturally he is hard on it and sweeps it aside.

Then, on the other hand, he gets over the hump of vital truth-claims by categorizing the doctrines of all the faiths as resulting from revelation and true for communion with God, though not, it seems, cognitively significant. With this understanding, so he urges, inter-faith dialogue will become simply an exploring of each other's religious experiences, which is what we all most need.

We return now to his story line, to see how he makes his case. Step one (chapters 3–6) is to dismiss three currently advocated views that do not measure up to his proposal. These chapters are somewhat oblique, because the reasons he gives for rejecting each view are in no case the reason that clearly weighs most with him, namely that each of these views, as stated by its exponents, leaves the question of truth still on the table. They are interesting, however, for what they reveal of Michael's mind.

Exclusivism is his label for the view, taken straight from John 14:6, that the Lord Jesus Christ is "the way, the truth, and the life" for the world, and that none come to know "the Father" as their Father save by a living link with Jesus, either in the church's sacramental life (so Roman Catholicism) or through personal faith (so evangelicalism). Michael insinuates that John 14:6 may be an unauthentic anti-Jewish product of "the

Johannine community" (p. 80) rather than a word of Jesus himself, and finally rejects exclusivism because it envisages God condemning good people only because they have not heard of Jesus Christ. (This is incorrect: as Romans 1–3 shows, God condemns for sin, and all are sinners. Michael misrepresents.)

Inclusivism is Michael's label for the view that, true as John 14:6 is, honest seekers after God in non-Christian religions may receive Christ's salvation even though they lack factual knowledge about Jesus (so Vatican II, and some Protestants whom Michael does not mention). He rejects inclusivism because it is imperialistic toward other faiths and reversible in argument (i.e., a Muslim could claim that some Christians enjoy the favor of Allah though they do not know him as Muslims do). (Why this should worry Michael, in light of his overall position, is not clear to me, but it is hardly important.)

Pluralism is Michael's label for the position of John Hick and others, that a plurality of religions is God's will for mankind. This much is his own view too, but he faults the pluralism that others expound for its inability to distinguish good and healthy beliefs from those that are neither, and for seeming to say that all beliefs of all religions are equally true—a notion that discourages serious commitment to any of them.

Step two starts with a renewed plea for religious partnership (chapter 7), which becomes a springboard for projecting the idea that in all religions the same core reality is contacted in experiences of mystical—that is, *trans-rational*—meditation and prayer (chapter 8). Michael draws on Hinduism, the Buddha, and three Christians—Eckhart, Mechtild, and Merton—to illustrate this, and ends the chapter asking whether, walking in their footsteps, we can today find a "breakthrough point in our own faith journey beyond which there lies the possibility of an enormous spiritual freedom,

deeper global understanding, and a more elevated communion with God?" (p. 117).

In chapter 9, this question is in effect answered as Michael
profiles Frithjof Schuon's so-called esoteric, whom clearly he
sees as a person living this higher-quality life. We are now at
the climactic point of the book's argument, so we shall linger
here a little.

Schuon, says Michael, has been acclaimed (by whom, I
wonder?) as "the greatest living authority on comparative
religions" (p. 119), and so he may be, but his views as Michael
describes, and apparently endorses them, make him sound like
some sort of occultist. He posits a transcendent Reality, the
Truth, in which all religions find their unity, but it is beyond
time, history, and human knowledge. Religions "are the finite
and relative vehicles by which this Truth is known by human
beings—and also the means by which Truth knows itself"
(p. 119). All religions are particular forms of the Truth revealing
itself in culture-specific contexts. So, for Schuon, "Jesus is the
true revelation of God. He does not contest ... that 'He is
the reflection of God's glory, the exact imprint of God's very
being' (Heb 1:3). Nor does he disagree with the same claim made
by Hindus about the many incarnations of Vishnu, or with the
Muslim belief that the divine will is fully revealed in the Qur'an.
For he treats all of these forms as intermediate self-disclosures
of the Absolute, which are necessarily final from the human
standpoint but necessarily relative from God's" (p. 121).

Michael continues to act as Schuon's prophet in his next
paragraph. The reason why revelation has to be mediated
rather than direct, and multi-form rather than limited to one
single demonstration, in Schuon's view, is that the human mind
is incapable of receiving the Absolute in its pure essence. For
our limited nature to be connected to the unmediated Absolute

would be like connecting a light bulb directly to a nuclear power station. The result would be disastrous: "If Christ had been the only manifestation of the Word, supposing such a uniqueness of manifestation to be possible, the effect of His birth would have been the instantaneous reduction of the universe to ashes." Thus Schuon argues that a diversity of revelation from the divine to the human, the observed variety of the world's religions, is not only genuine but absolutely necessary. "The world could not tolerate a single vehicle of access to the Absolute. It would destroy the fabric of creation" (p. 121).

The fact that Michael evidently wants his readers to embrace this Gnostic occultism is daunting, to say the least.

But we proceed. Alongside the above cosmology, or metaphysic, or myth, or whatever we should call it, Schuon, through Michael, now offers us a religious typology of the entire human race. As in Gilbert's jingle every boy and every gal that's born into the world alive is either a little Liberal, or else a little Conservative, so every religious person, says Schuon, is either an exoteric or an esoteric. Exoterics like specifics and precision, and find finality in facts; for them, "abstractions and universalities have no grasp on the imagination or on the heart" (p. 122). Esoterics, by contrast, see facts as symbols and look beyond them to what is symbolized. For them "the particular elements of religious faith are not of significance in themselves except as they reveal the hidden God within and behind them. The esoteric is drawn beyond the particular to the universal, the Absolute that transcends and relativizes the specific.... In this state of awareness, historical and material distinctions are of little value. The ways in which God can be known are endless" (p. 122).

Michael does not say whether it is better to be an esoteric than an exoteric, but clearly he thinks it is, for only esoterics can easily tune in to what he and Schuon are affirming about religions. Whether Michael thinks that natural-born exoterics can become esoterics by disciplined mental exercise he also does not say; it seems that he doubts it, yet hopes they will try, even though as unreconstructed exoterics they still have a contribution to make to inter-faith dialogue (pp. 123–24). But he insists that both esoterics and exoterics must approach the dialogue from a position of "grounded openness"— "grounded," that is, in the ongoing life of a "faith community," and "open" to detect divine grace in the practitioners and procedures of other religious groups.

Step three, set out in chapter 10, "Drawing the Circle Wider," is to round off the argument by urging us to see the maintaining of historic Christian exclusivism today as a case of arrested development, the spiritual equivalent of an infantile fixation, and to recognize the pluralism of the inter-faith movement as a new stage in the world's religious evolution, truly the wave of the future and one that is fully compatible with Christ and Scripture though not envisaged in either. So we should stop worrying about whether people are saved and give ourselves to our proper task in the modern world, namely philanthropic service of suffering humanity.

THE CRITIQUE

There are in life many no-win situations, and being a revisionist Anglican bishop is one of them. A bishop's job description, as defined in Anglican ordinals and in the expectations of Anglican people, includes declaring and defending the Christian faith as the Anglican Church has received it. The prestige of bishops in their dioceses remains enormous; people treat them as gurus, and so find it deeply traumatic when their bishop says things that seem wrong. The troubled episcopates of E. W. Barnes, J. A. T. Robinson, and David Jenkins in England, and of John Spong in New Jersey, amply illustrate this. Because Anglicans show courtesy and restraint when dealing with bishops, the revisionists do not always see how much of an upset they are causing, or how great are the pastoral problems they create by undermining people's confidence in their wisdom and getting out of step with those they lead; and because the revisionists, like other bishops, have power to manage their dioceses more or less as they please, they are tempted to think that the disagreements about Christian truth which they generate as they go along have no domestic significance. In fact, however, a diocese is put under great strain when its bishop flaunts dissent from established Anglican ways. It is to be hoped that Bishop Michael, sensitive man that he is, is coming to realize this.

Meantime, how should we assess *Mansions*? Words of appreciation first. Michael's passion for worldwide peace, socioeconomic, political, and religious, is something to admire and emulate. The inter-religious hatred and mayhem that have disfigured world history, and still disfigure it, should draw tears from us all, and Michael's strong repudiation of both is entirely proper. The global ethic of tolerance, non-violence, truthfulness, honesty, justice, equality, respect for human rights, and mutual care, which Hans Küng formulated in 1993 and which Michael applauds and prints as an appendix, is a superb statement of what are, in fact, Christian community standards for our agonized and agonizing world. And though it is doubtful whether any form of inter-faith dialogue could make as much difference to the human condition as Michael hopes, while his own rules for it involve insuperable difficulties, as we shall see, he is right to urge that for people of various religions to talk together is a worthwhile exercise that broadens and deepens.

He is right, therefore, to encourage us all to practice inter-religious dialogue as, when, and where we can.

But *Mansions* presents profound problems. In it, Michael tries to ride two horses. There is a happy sight gag in the film *On Golden Pond* where a not-quite-admirable young man stands nonchalantly with one foot on the jetty and one in the boat; boat and jetty part company, arms flail, and into the pond he goes with what to the viewer is a satisfying splash. Michael, unhappily, has located himself in a comparable position. The boat of his principled pluralism proves, on inspection, to have drifted away from the jetty of historic Christianity, and self-contradictory double-talk results. This is in no way satisfying; on the contrary, it is distressing. But the diagnosis is unavoidable. Trying to ride two horses at once, Michael comes to grief.

On the one hand, presenting himself as a spokesman for the global hopes and dreams of the cluster of organized groups that make up the inter-faith movement, he embraces, as we have seen, a pluralism that declares all major religions true in the sense in which Christianity is true—that is (for so Michael uses the word) genuinely effective for putting people in touch with God. In this sense all are true; none are false. Michael's claim has the effect of setting them all on a level with Christianity, and of placing their founders and gurus on a par with Jesus, and of classifying Christianity as one of the many disciplines available for realizing contact with the transcendent Ultimate. Contrasts between concepts of the Ultimate, and of contact with it, so Michael declares, reflect cultural conditioning only: there is no real divergence. On Schuon's authority, Michael hints that exoterics, being matter-of-fact people, will note these contrasts and be unable to conceive that there is convergence here; esoterics, however, treating doctrines simply as symbols, will not have that difficulty and will discern the oneness of major religions with comparative ease.

Michael sees this mutual affirmation of religions as the completion of the process begun when Amos, Isaiah, and later prophets turned Israel's polytheism into monotheism and continued when Jesus and his apostles transmuted Israel's covenantal exclusivity into covenantal universality. (This account of the biblical process seems a bit skewed, but we leave that for the moment.) Michael declares that "God's continuing revelation" in the church sometimes takes us "beyond the Bible," and in this case "the new global context of religious and cultural pluralism requires new acts of biblical interpretation"—by which he means affirming some things Scripture does not affirm and denying some things it does (p. 135). This is one side of his thought.

On the other hand, writing as a Christian leader, Michael insists that none of this "should be taken as a denial or relativizing of the truth of Christ" (p. 137), or as calling in question his own commitment to Christ and to evangelism, or as damping down his desire that all whom he addresses should share that commitment. "A Christian is one who believe Jesus to be the way, the truth and the life." (How good to find Michael saying this, after querying the authenticity of John 14:6!—see pp. 59, 80.) "This is not to say that there are no others [i.e., ways that are truth and life]. It is to say simply that it is the one we know. And for that reason it is the path we must follow and invite others along" (p. 138). "Any who seek the fullness of life, and who desire to be rescued from broken lives of sin and self-concern, all who long for pardon, forgiveness, hope and joy, need only turn to him [Jesus] and God will do the rest" (p. 140). This is the other side of his thought.

Michael's Christology is elusive. As he speaks of "the gospel" without defining it, so he speaks of "the person and work of Christ" without telling us what he takes either to be (p. 138). He doubts the authenticity of Jesus' recorded witness to his unity with the Father (p. 59). He speaks of the "many incarnations of Vishnu" in Hindu myths (p. 121) but nowhere applies that word to Jesus, and he parades before us (granted, without himself endorsing) the anti-incarnationalism of John Hick (p. 82). He writes like one whose mind is in the toils of what, in the theologians' world, is called Spirit-Christology or degree-Christology, which tries to explain the Word becoming flesh as a special case of the indwelling of the Spirit of God in a fine man. Yet Michael's purpose of affirming the reality and divine authority of Jesus, the living Lord, seems clear, and in that we rejoice.

But this is where the trouble starts. If Bishop Michael was only saying that Jesus was one of humankind's many insightful religious teachers, and that turning to him today is like turning to Socrates, or Gandhi, or the Buddha—fixing one's mind, that is, on an inspiring historical instance of the kind of wisdom and nobility to which one aspires—there would be a problem, to be sure, about his Christianity, but none about his consistency. His evident intention of expressing more than this, however, raises the problem of his consistency in an acute way, as we shall now see.

After a century and a half of sustained skeptical testing by professional academics of the New Testament account of things, certain facts can fairly be said to be established beyond the possibility of rational denial. (That does not mean that denials of them by non-Christians, anti-Christians, and deviant Christians will now cease; it simply means that the unreasonableness of such denials can, from now on, always be made evident.) Indisputably, the Christian church from the start proclaimed Jesus of Nazareth, crucified, risen, reigning, and returning, as God's Christ, the divinely promised Messiah, the center of world history, now from his throne imparting his transforming power and presence to his people through the Pentecostal Holy Spirit. Indisputably, apostolic Christianity was not only a message about personal salvation and supernatural living in the church, the home, and the body politic, but was also a philosophy of history celebrating an imperial Lord who came the first time in humility to bear away sin and would reappear in majesty to judge all humankind and to bring final bliss to his born-again followers. Indisputably, Christians from the start prayed to this Jesus and, in due course, found words to express the initially unthinkable thought of his personal divinity within the being of God. Indisputably too (*pace* John Hick and Bishop Michael, p. 82) all this had its roots in the teaching of Jesus himself as the apostles remembered, relayed, and recorded it. Attempts to drive a wedge between Jesus and his apostles boomerang, for what becomes clear eventually every time is the solidarity of the four gospels with the rest of the New Testament literature.

Also indisputably, the bottom line of the apostolic proclamation of the universal dominion of Jesus the Christ was Jesus' claim on the allegiance of the entire human race. Jesus, risen, was believed to have told his apostles: "Go and make disciples of all nations, baptizing them ... and teaching them to obey everything I have commanded you" (Matt 28:19-20). Accordingly, in a world of religious pluralism at least as complex as ours, converts "turned to God from idols to serve the living and true God, and to wait for his Son from heaven, whom he raised from the dead—Jesus, who rescues us from the coming wrath" (1 Thess 1:9-10). For they were taught that they must acknowledge the exclusive, permanent, all-embracing lordship of Jesus Christ, the eternal Savior-Judge to whom all authority has been given, and must therefore forsake all contrary forms of religious belief and practice.

This apostolic presentation of what used to be called "the crown rights of the Redeemer" has been shaping the church for two millennia. All the martyrdoms, from the first to the twentieth century, of those who would not be involved in official paganisms, and all the missionary outreach there has ever been, were expressions of loyalty to Jesus Christ the Lord, thus understood. For this apostolic teaching claims to be non-negotiable revealed truth—truth, not just in Michael's functional sense of producing the experience it promises, but in the everyday sense of statements corresponding to fact and telling us what is the case and how things actually are. Any declaration that is ever true in this sense will go on being true till the facts themselves change, and since it is basic to apostolic Christianity to declare that "Jesus Christ is the same yesterday and today and for ever" (Heb 13:8), the apostolic affirmation that the Lord Jesus Christ claims everyone's exclusive submission and allegiance must be held to be still valid.

To legitimize non-Christian religions, therefore, and set them on a par with Christianity, as pluralism does, is to part company with the apostolic faith of the New Testament at a very deep level. John Hick realized this and spoke of his own shift from inclusivism to pluralism as the crossing of a Rubicon, in a way that involved a Copernican revolution in his theology. One wishes everyone saw the matter so clearly. Whatever guesses we think it right to make about divine grace to seeking souls who never heard of Christ, and however much we admire the poise and good-heartedness we see in some adherents of other religions, the crown rights of the Redeemer are non-negotiable. The Lord Jesus Christ, the incarnate Son of God, must be proclaimed not only as the all-sufficient Savior of everyone who trusts him, but also as all humankind's rightful and exclusive Master.

So it must sadly be said that Bishop Michael's generous proposal that all the great religions—Hinduism, Buddhism, Judaism, Islam, Taoism, Confucianism, and the rest—be acknowledged as belonging to God's loving plan for their own cultural worlds, and as mediating the same grace that Christians receive through Christ, so that conversion from them is needless, is an idea for which there is neither basis nor room. It is ruled out by the lordship-claim of Jesus Christ. Michael is right to say that rubbing shoulders with persons of different religions, and appreciating what they have devotionally, is an enriching thing to do, but his idea that a legitimized plurality of religions was what God aimed at all along must be rated a fantasy, and his wish that some should receive the apostolic Christ as Savior in the context of his negating of the apostolic insistence that all should receive him as Lord, because that is what he is, must be judged a gross inconsistency.

Is Michael's Jesus Christ the Christ of apostolic faith, of the New Testament and the creeds, and of historical Anglicanism, or not? When we hear of the Christ who saves the needy that turn to him, it seems that the answer is yes; but when we realize that we are being told of a Christ who is not and will never be Lord of all, because religious pluralism is his Father's plan, it seems that the answer is no. One cannot have it both ways, so what is the answer really?

Practical situations bring out the significance of theoretical positions, so consider the following:

While in India some years ago, I met with a well-read Hindu gentleman who worked for the government. His wife was a Christian, and a friend had been sharing Christian faith with him for some time; he was clearly feeling torn between the claims of the Christ of the New Testament (that is—let me say it explicitly—the *real* Christ), and the Hinduism of his upbringing, which for social reasons he did not want to leave. He opened the conversation by producing a cutting from India's national daily and asking for my comments on it. It was a report of a speech by Archbishop Runcie, in which he expressed delight that India was so religious a country, and said that had he been born in India he had no doubt he would have been a Hindu, and implied that that would have been entirely satisfactory. Bishop Michael's principles, I think, would have required me to say that Runcie's attitude was right, that the ethnic distribution of religions in different parts of the world was to be seen as part of God's plan, and that Hinduism gives its adherents what Christ gives Christians, so that my inter-locutor's anxiety as to whether he should change his religion might safely be laid to rest. What I actually did, following prin-ciples that had earlier been focused for me by Bishop Stephen Neill, and that have recently been advocated by Bishop Lesslie Newbigin, another veteran of Indian mission service, was tell him that, though I hated having to disagree with the head of the Anglican Communion, I thought Runcie was quite wrong; and I spoke about the person and place of Christ, and his univer-sal claim on us, much as I have done in this critique. I was not being imperialist or superior (Michael's words); I was simply trying to be obedient and faithful, and of benefit to my neigh-bor. I do not know how this gentleman's story ended, but he seemed to find force in what I was saying, and at his request we had another conversation along similar lines before I left. Did I act properly? I believe so.

To make my position fully clear, I need now to state my answers to two questions that are constantly asked me with regard to non-Christian religions.

First, do their adherents worship the God Christians worship? Yes and no. *Yes*, in the sense that God the Creator, the only God there is, who reveals himself to Christians through the Word incarnate and the written words of Scripture, imparts to all humans inklings of his divine reality, of his standards and guardianship of morality, and of his goodwill to mankind as such. Theologians label the many aspects of this process general revelation. All non-Christian religions have grown out of general revelation as their seed-bed, with many cultural factors coming in to give them their present shape. No, for, to start with, non-Christian religions know nothing about the triunity of God and the incarnation of the Son, and the inklings spoken of, refracted through fallen minds, regularly become so diminished and distorted that the object of worship is unrecognizable, in character terms, as the God and Father of our Lord Jesus Christ. Paul lays all this out briefly in Romans 1 and 2.

Second, do non-Christian religions mediate the same grace as is known to Christian believers?

Bishop Michael, as we have seen, thinks yes; I can only say that I have no reason to agree with him, either from what I know of the religions by reading and observation or from the witness of people I know who were nurtured in them before finding Christ. An ex-Hindu friend wept in England's General Synod as he spoke against a moratorium on missionary evangelism, contrasting the light and life Christ had brought him with the oppressive darkness of what he had known before. While taking Michael's point that religions should be compared at their best and not otherwise, I suspect that his top-level inter-faith experience, allied to his political dream of worldwide inter-faith solidarity and his personal recoil from his former proud lack of interest in other faiths as described in chapter 1, has left him more starry-eyed about the richness of non-Christian religion than the facts warrant.

Certainly, it is only Christians who know a God whose love for individuals led him to give his Son to die in the worst agony ever in order to bring them to himself; it is only Christians who know a divine-human Savior, the hands and side of whose risen body bear permanent scars from his cross, who by his Spirit walks with his followers to a heavenly home where they will enjoy his love for ever; it is only Christians who know a Holy Spirit who renews twisted hearts and transforms perverted dispositions into the likeness of Jesus' own heart of holiness and love; and it is only Christians who know that they have passed from death into life, and will never come under condemnation, since another's righteousness and sacrificial death cover all their faults for eternity. No other religion has ever offered anything like this cluster of blessings, so if non-Christians are strangers to such grace it should cause no surprise. It seems, after all, that real love of neighbor, no less than loyalty to the real Christ, requires even in our changing modern world continuance of Christ-centered missionary outreach everywhere.

At the start of this discussion we heard the past Archbishop of Canterbury, Robert Runcie, advocating the approach that *Mansions* follows. As we close, I would like us to hear the present Archbishop of Canterbury, George Carey, on the same topic.

I have become alarmed by the growth of what I call religious pluralism in First World Churches. I mean by this a shift of focus from a Trinitarian faith anchored in the centrality of Christ to a vague, amorphous belief in God in which Christ is not the definitive focus, but only one of many foci of faith.... Such faith needs the blood transfusion that can only come through an unapologetic and firm, historic faith.

Again:

One of the most disturbing trends in the Western Church has been a tendency for some to loosen their grip on the singularity of Jesus Christ. We have been bullied into this by powerful theological voices which have suggested that Christianity must come to terms with its own "parochiality." It has no right to challenge Islam or any other religion. It is merely the Western face of God. It must therefore surrender its commitment to being accepted in every part of the world and be content to be one fact and one voice among many. This view is to be rejected firmly. Of course, we hear and respond to those who resist the militaristic methods of some evangelism.... But to be concerned for these things does not mean we cease therefore, to proclaim the uniqueness of Christ. To do so is a denial both of our history and our theology. (Cited from *The Anglican Digest*, Lent 1995, pp. 33, 63)

It has been no pleasure to record my dissent from my diocesan bishop's published views. It was delightful to receive from him last Christmas a card on the front of which were the Magi on camels and the legend: "The Wise Seek Him Still."

With the words of the Archbishop of Canterbury, and of Bishop Michael's Christmas card, I could not agree more.

CHAPTER 3

CHRIST, THE CHURCH, AND THE PARLIAMENT OF WORLD RELIGIONS

Ron Dart

For one of the most ancient principles of their constitution is religious toleration ... everyone was free to practice what religion he liked, and to try and convert other people to his faith, provided he did it quietly and politely, by rational argument. But, if he failed to convince them, he was not allowed to make bitter attacks on other religions, nor to employ violence or personal abuse.

—Thomas More
Utopia (1516) Bk. II

I am no pluralist; I am a Catholic.

—Hans Urs Von Balthasar

There can be no doubt that we live at a time when all the major and minor religions of the world meet and greet one another on a regular basis. It is still possible to retreat into isolation, but for those who take their faith with any seriousness, such a position is not an option. The era of the Christendom model has come to an end, as has modernity itself (dominated by science and a one-dimensional methodology). This new reality in the West has resulted in an immense openness to religion and spirituality. How is the church to make sense of the vast diversity and compelling pluralism of faith communities in our ever-present global village? Should we see ourselves as a part of a circle of voices, a religious tapestry, a rainbow coalition, or a perspective within the ever-growing Parliament of World's Religions? Is Jesus the Christ merely one manifestation of the Divine or, as God incarnate, is he distinct from Hindu avatars and Buddhist bodhisattvas? In short, are all the major founders and important teachers of world religions merely equal but different physicians of the soul? Is the church one means of expressing the Divine or, as a Divine society, are its myths, symbols, liturgies, purposes, and aims on a different level than a mosque, gurdwara, pogoda, ashram, or synagogue? Do such historic claims by the church lead to imperialism, intolerance, and arrogance, or are there other ways of understanding the message of Christ, the church, and the world? These sorts of questions will not go away. The task before us is to explore the various ways and means of answering them.

OUR GLOBAL VILLAGE, PLURALISM, AND INTER-FAITH DIALOGUE

The Lambeth Conference (1988) published a timely pamphlet on this challenging subject entitled *Towards a Theology for Inter-Faith Dialogue*. True to the tradition of not unduly offending anyone, it speaks in the language of "towards," "dialogue," "exploration," "beginnings," "journey," "pilgrimage," and "provisional thinking" on this controversial topic. We must never denigrate the tentative and suggestive nature of such large and complex issues, but such an approach to inter-faith dialogue can too easily get mired in process and procedure and become, tragically, soft on substantive content. The reaction to this more hesitant liberal approach, with its proper respect for uncertainty, the "God beyond God" and the "Divine Mystery," is often a pinched and narrow fundamentalism in which all theology must be about clear, distinct, and absolute views of God and many other things. Liberals and fundamentalists, often, spend much of their waking hours reacting to one another. The position taken by the Lambeth Conference walks the extra mile to acknowledge the valid insights of other faith traditions (and rightly so), but it runs the risk, in doing so, of leveling the religious playing field. The fact that we live in an "inter-spiritual age" cannot be denied, but are all forms of spiritual theology equally valid? *Towards a Theology for Inter-Faith Dialogue* raises many key questions, but the hesitancy of the pamphlet tends to be both its strength and weakness.

We live at a period of time when mysticism, spirituality, myth, narrative, symbol, and the esoteric have been given preferred status to theology and the institutions of the major and minor religions of the world. This is a cultural reaction, of course, to the way theology has been taken captive by Cartesian rationalism and the means by which religious institutions have often betrayed their high calling. But, as a reaction, it has a limited life expectancy. Those who assume that they can falsely and artificially sever spirituality and theology fail to see that as soon as they open their mouths they are doing theology. We are in a desperate need for a solid mystical theology rather than a reactive pluralist pietism that uncritically assumes an "ersatz" and uprooted interest in some sort of vague "spirituality" will answer the deepest longings of the human heart, head, and culture.

The recent publication of Bishop Michael Ingham's *Mansions of the Spirit*, yet once again, opens up for us important issues that must be addressed. We must not flinch from entering and being challenged by our multi-faith context; there is much to be learned from the wisdom of other religious traditions. *Mansions of the Spirit* is a rather popular apologetic for "the Primordial tradition" and the inter-faith movement that began with the first Parliament of World's Religions in 1893 and culminated in a second Parliament in 1993. Ingham probes four models for inter-faith dialogue in *Mansions of the Spirit*: exclusive, inclusive, pluralist, syncretist. The conclusion of the book tends to waffle between a sort of critical pluralism and transcendent syncretism, and it is difficult to sort out where Ingham finally plants his flag. The fact that *Mansions of the Spirit* and the recent comments by the Moderator of the United Church of Canada (see *Macleans*, Dec. 15, 1997) point toward a rethinking of the historic Christian tradition that needs to be examined in some depth and detail. Are we bringing Trojan horses into the camp?

The rest of this paper will examine four main models of inter-faith dialogue. The exclusive, inclusive, pluralist, and syncretist paradigms will be explored from different angles. Each model contributes important insights and ways of doing inter-faith dialogue, but each model, also, has certain limitations, dark and shadow sides. We need to realize that all of these approaches are merely human creations (or constructs), and we should not bow uncritically to any of them; to do so is to worship an idol. Tribalists will often uncritically genuflect before one of the paradigms while being keen and eager to ferret out weak spots and problems in other models. I hope we will be able to see the attractions and deficiencies of each approach to inter-faith dialogue, and by doing so, be able to know how to engage both our own tradition and other traditions in a challenging yet respectful manner.

THE EXCLUSIVE APPROACH

The *exclusive* model has, unfortunately, received the worst press, and if it is interpreted in a certain way, it deserves strong criticism. Often, exclusivism is crudely equated with some of the worst forms of fundamentalism or cultic movements. There is no doubt that the exclusive model can degenerate to this level, but those who only see the model in this manner have not looked too far or deep. The exclusive perspective is often used as an example of how Christianity goes into other cultures, and in the name of bringing Christ to a foreign land and culture, maims, destroys, and negates much that is good in it. All sorts of horror stories are regularly and routinely pulled out of the ample bag of history to illustrate the dangers and dark side of a foolish missionary position. *The Missionaries: God Against the Indians* (1988), by N. Lewis, and the more challenging, *The Missionary Position: Mother Teresa in Theory and Practice* (1995), by C. Hitchens, illustrate many legitimate concerns about an uncritical view of exclusivism. It must be noted, though, that the exclusive tendencies in other religions have perpetuated their own sorts of horrors on Christians and many others. M. Marty's extensive work on *The Fundamentalist Project* and his equally superb book, *Fundamentalisms Observed* (1991), have provided an up-to-date compendium of the dangers of various types of the exclusivist model gone amuck and astray in many religions. It is, also, important to note the exclusivist way of thinking and acting in our broader secular context. We do not need to look too far into the heart of the twentieth century to see how secular exclusivists have wreaked havoc (probably much more than any other religious group) in all sorts of areas.

So, a word of caution—the notion that *my* tribe is right, other clans are wrong, and it is my task (through persuasion or force) to make others see this truth runs through culture wars, economics, politics, education, ethnic cleansing, nationalism, and patriotism, not just religion.

We need to realize, then, that the exclusive model, in the wrong hands, can be used to create a mood and climate of intolerance and fear. This model has been used, by the powerful and proud, to serve all sorts of imperial interests. Those who would deny this reality or those who are blind to the way this approach can be misused need to ponder the potential way the exclusive model can be used for demonic ends. But, there is much more to this model than the litany of abuses listed above. I might just add that those who can only see the exclusive paradigm through tinted and negative eyeglasses just might be missing much. We need to ask ourselves, then, about the positive aspect of this approach and why, in many ways, it is the most persistent and perennial in most religious traditions.

Karl Barth, without much doubt, was one of the major theologians of the twentieth century; Barth's turn from the naive theological liberalism of the early part of this century did not take him into either the fundamentalist or evangelical tribes. The neo-orthodoxy of Barth was centered and grounded in the redemptive power of the risen Christ; Barth's commentary on Romans is a classic work of exegesis in this troubled century. Barth, without a doubt, was both an exclusivist, and to the surprise of many, a universalist. Barth firmly believed that Jesus the Christ, as God incarnate, excluded all other gurus, messiahs, avatars, and bodhisattvas from having the final word, but "in Christ" all were included. Barth and Bonhoeffer's view of Christ meant that Fascism and National Socialism had to be exorcized and excluded from the meaning of the gospel. Barth was equally quick, after the war, to recognize that the prophetic work of W. Stringfellow in the United States excluded the "Pax Americana" from sitting on the same throne as Christ. So, in all sorts of ways, Christ and the church exclude the pretensions of all sorts of political and economic messiahs. But, let us take the issue from the ethical to the metaphysical level.

Judaism excluded Christianity for the simple reason that both groups understood who Jesus the Christ was and is in different ways. If Jesus was merely a prophet or rabbi, I suspect, the stark differences between Judaism and Christianity could have been minimized. Islam is different from both Judaism and Christianity because it sees itself as the consummation and historic fulfillment of both. Needless to say, Christianity and Judaism tend to differ with the way the Qur'an plays fast and loose with their traditions. Gabriel's message to Muhammad about Jesus tends to conflict with the Christian community's interpretation of who Jesus was, is, and ever shall be. Who is right and who is wrong? The fact that the answers to these sorts of questions create communities that exclude one another raises issues that will not leave us. The Oriental traditions are not excluded from the same issues even though some Romantic Westerners tend to think so. The mystical monism of some of the *Upanishads* is quite different from and excludes the mystical theism of the *Svetasvatara Upanishad* and the *Gita* (by reducing the personalist approach to a lower level of religious knowledge). Sankara and Ramanuja, as leading Hindu mystics, tend to see and articulate their understanding of the Ultimate in different ways. Is the goal of the religious life a *unio mystica* between the soul and God (comparable to the connatural union of two lovers) or does the Self dissolve like salt in water by being absorbed into the Ultimate? These positions do exclude one another. Early Hinayana-Theravada Buddhism, like Jainism, took a strong stance against both the mystical monism and theism of classical Hinduism; these traditions tended to be silent about the reality of a Divine Being, and their notion of the Self (if there was such a thing?) was quite distinct and different from Hinduism. The dialogue between T. Merton and D. T. Suzuki in *Zen and the Birds of Appetite* highlights how Zen Buddhism and Catholic Christianity have important points of convergence, but these traditions do part company at a certain point on the trail; that is, they do exclude one another. Is the Christian view of eternal life the same as the Buddhist notion of *nirvana*? The deeper one probes these distinctions, the more points of concord and discord appear. The Mahayana tradition, with its respect for a personal god (Amida) is quite different from the Hinayana stance. These two traditions within Buddhism do exclude one another at a certain point.

I could go on with these sorts of comparisons and contrasts for pages, but I think the point has been made. The mystical theologians both within and between traditions do differ on both what the religious Ultimate is like (or even if there is an Ultimate), and the nature and means of transformation from the illusory, conscious, or old self to the new being (if there is such a thing). The fact that these differences do exist should not be minimized or ignored; this stubborn reality means that some sort of exclusion is built into the very nature of the human quest to receive, articulate, and live forth a vision of the renewed life.

Does the exclusive model, inevitably and necessarily, lead to intolerance and contempt for other religions? Those who assume it does need to think much deeper about the issue. Authentic and genuine dialogue means being thoroughly rooted and grounded in a tradition and speaking from it.

Traditions do exclude one another, but tolerance and respect only begin when we face the other, disagree on the deepest issues, yet continue to honor the "thou-ness" of the other. I think it can be argued that the most profound understanding of tolerance rises from the traditions in which the exclusive model has the deepest hold.

It is, also, quite true to most traditions to argue, when all the cards are put on the table, one exclusivist position trumps the other. Those who ignore this persistent reality or attempt (with the best of pluralist intentions) to interpret this reality in a way that glosses over abiding differences distort the meaning of dialogue.

THE INCLUSIVE (CATHOLIC) MODEL

If the exclusive model has a tendency to highlight the point of divergence and discord within and between religious traditions, the *inclusive* model has a passion to find as many points of concord and convergence as possible. The inclusive approach is interested in how God's abundant grace, in and through Christ, fulfills and crowns the noblest strivings, longings, and aspirations of other religions and cultures. The so-called "fulfillment thesis" can be found in the earliest forms of Christian writings. The New Testament book of Hebrews argues that all of the Jewish symbols and history anticipate and prefigure the advent of Christ; hence Jesus the Christ is the fulfillment of Judaism. Needless to say, the Jews did not agree with such a thesis. St. John uses the same approach to the classical Greek and Roman culture of the time with his Logos theology. Greek and Roman philosophic, mystical, and theological thought had a high view of the eternal *logos*; John argued that Jesus was the *logos* incarnate. Again, we see the "grace crowning nature" approach at work. The Alexandrian school of Christianity (Clement and

Origen), and most of the patristic approach (West and East) argued that just as Judaism was a preparation and prologue to Christianity for the Jews, so also Greek and Roman philosophy anticipated and was fulfilled in Christ. This inclusive or *catholic* model can be found in S. Weil's *Intimations of Christianity Amongst the Early Greeks*; Weil followed the same approach in her study of Oriental religions. The inclusive method was used by E. Stanley Jones in *Gandhi: Portrayal of a Friend*, B. Griffith's *The Marriage of East and West*, Wee-Chong Tan's *Lao Tzu and Gandhi (Friends of Jesus)*, and J. Douglass's *Lightning East to West: Jesus, Gandhi, and the Nuclear Age*. The ongoing dialogue between Christianity and other religious traditions, at its best, seeks to find points of common ground. B. Epperly does much the same thing with New Age spirituality in *Crystal and Cross: Christians and New Age in Creative Dialogue*. The inclusive approach, then, seeks to discern how God has been active in other traditions through general revelation, but holds that in Christ natural theology finds its fullest expression.

The inclusive method is keenly aware of much of the bad press of the exclusive approach to inter-faith dialogue, and those who use this model work overtime to bridge chasms that need not exist. The inclusive model, though, can be used by other traditions as well. These traditions argue that their view of the Ultimate crowns and fulfills Christianity. Islam, for example, is quick to find the best and finest insights in Judaism and Christianity, but, when day is done, the Muslims see their tradition as a fulfillment of the noblest longings of other traditions. G. Parrinder's *Jesus in the Qur'an* highlights in detail how the Islamic tradition, in the Qur'an, interprets Jesus to suit its fulfillment thesis. It is little help to argue that the Muslim mystics (Sufis) see things in a much different way; none of them argue that union with Christ is the fulfillment of Islam. Bahai, with its *syncretist* approach, sees itself as the crown and fulfillment of many of the major and minor religions of the world; obviously, followers of these traditions differ with the way Bahai plays fast and loose with texts and traditions. *The Hindu View of Life*, by Radhakrishnan, is true to the fulfillment thesis, but the position taken by Radhakrishnan is that neo-Vedantic Hinduism is the highest level of religious understanding, and all other approaches are lower, lesser, inferior, or subordinate forms of religious understanding. The inclusive model, then, ranks different levels of religious knowledge based on a prior understanding of ultimate reality. In short, the inclusive model can be and has been used by many religious traditions to prioritize their perspective while walking the extra mile to honor and respect the finest insights of other traditions.

It is important to recognize, then, that the appeal of the inclusive model is that it seeks to find common ground within and between religious traditions, but there comes a point when one tradition is preferred in comparison to another. In short, the inclusive method starts from the position that the preferred tradition includes the best of other traditions, but the final word on the Ultimate (and the means to reach it) belongs to one group rather than another. This does not mean, of course, that God's grace is only restricted to the Christian tradition. The medieval theologians made the distinction between *de potentia ordinate* and *de potentia absoluta*; the ordained means of grace is in and through the "one, holy, catholic and apostolic church" (*notae ecclesiae*), but God's absolute power can bypass such ordained means of grace. The inclusive model within the Christian tradition, just as in other traditions, excludes, by reducing other traditions to a lower level of understanding, but God's absolute power and love is greater than the ordained means of grace. Many argue that the inclusive approach can be rather patronizing to those who are lower on the scale of religious insight, and there is some truth in such a concern. R. Panikkar's *The Unknown Christ of Hinduism* (drawing from Rahner's notion of the anonymous Christian) was much welcomed as a superb work from a Christian inclusivist position, but many devoted Hindus were not impressed. A reply from the Hindu tradition to Panikkar might be entitled *The Unknown Brahman of Christianity*.

We need to ask, then, whether the inclusive model for interfaith dialogue best preserves a robust and healthy form of tolerance, or whether, at a certain juncture, the meaning of tolerance is negated by a patronizing stance. There is no doubt that the inclusive approach seeks for areas of concord, and this stance refuses to caricature other traditions; understanding and empathy is basic and a foundational way of seeing and being for the inclusivist. This is why, for example, spirituality and the contemplative way have played such a vital and vibrant role in this method. Merton, Griffiths, Keating, Main, Freeman, Graham, Johnston, McNamara, and Steunl-Rast have tried to be true to and reclaim the meditative approaches to God that have been kept on the margins in our hectic and productivity-oriented society. Many Catholic, Orthodox, Anglican, and an increasing number of Protestants are keen and eager to learn from ancient meditative traditions and walk their journey with spiritual directors and soul friends. It would be foolish and unduly reactive to ignore or downplay this important interest in spiritual practices; we should be grateful that the West is once again searching for its contemplative roots, and we should also be grateful that contemplatives from the East and West are learning from one another. The inclusivist and fully catholic way supports such a renewal of the depths of transformation.

But, once we move beyond various types of meditative techniques to the deeper purpose of such techniques, we need to ask, what is the end or purpose of such practices? This brings us into the core of mystical theology and the way different mystics interpret the process of transformation from the illusory ego to the new self. We inevitably face the stubborn fact that different religious traditions answer these questions in quite distinct ways, and the answers do collide. It is much wiser, then, to put all the big cards on the table at the beginning of the day. If, when day is done, the inclusive model presupposes that one tradition (at its best) is to be preferred to others, it is better to state this at the beginning. Does this mean nothing can be learned from other contemplative traditions? Of course not! The search for common ground and some sort of consensus is essential, but we need to discern when we have come to the end of dialogue; we also need to come clean about different understandings of what spirituality and contemplation mean. Again, true tolerance begins and ends when genuine points of discord, disagreement, and divergence are reached, but respect, civility, and charity dominate the day. The inclusive method, then, hinges on who is defining what is to be included, how wisdom and knowledge are to be ranked, and how such ranking does exclude some forms of insight from sitting on the throne. In short, an enlightened inclusivism goes a long way to soften religious differences, and such an approach offers a sound critique of a crude exclusivism. But, there comes a point when the inclusivist must draw boundaries and lines in the sand, and such a step means the demands of a sophisticated exclusivism must be faced and not flinched from.

THE PLURALIST MODEL

If the exclusive and inclusive paradigms both agree, in different ways and for different reasons, that ultimate reality can be known (regardless of how it is defined and known), the fans of *pluralism* beg to differ with such inflated notions. The pluralist model starts from the basic premise that the human mind and imagination are finite and fallible, prone to error and distraction, and incapable of thinking and speaking with final authority on ultimate concerns. The humanist tribe of the Enlightenment (unlike their secular cousins) did not want to banish religious longings and valid religious aspirations from the human heart and head. The humanist tradition merely sought to restrict and limit what could be known about the Divine. Men like Locke and Kant are very much the elder statesmen of our modern religious and broader cultural pluralism. The pluralist model, then, is not against the religious impulse; it merely refuses to grant any religious tradition preferred status. This model is grounded in the liberal idea of the autonomous individual, and the crucial role of conscience (it's all very Protestant), in defining what is religiously relevant and meaningful. Pluralism argues that intellectual humility asks of us that we do not tread on holy ground with an exaggerated sense of religious knowledge or feigned religious pronouncements or proclamations. The human mind is unable to faithfully hear, understand, interpret, and speak with any final authority on such divine mysteries. Tillich spoke of the "God beyond God," and Eckhart reminded his disciples and detractors that God is an Abyss, the Still Wilderness, the Nameless Nothing, and the Immoveable Rest. The Ultimate, in short, is beyond our ken, but we should respect and honor the various and varied mediators and intermediate manifestations between the Divine and our all too human and limited perceptions. This means, therefore, openness and tolerance, for the most part, to religious traditions, provided, of course, these traditions recognize their vision of the Ultimate is merely *their* vision.

Nathan the Wise, a dramatic and compelling play by G. Lessing, sums up this Enlightenment position in a graphic and telling way. Nathan is a Jew who must decide which religion is the truest and best (Judaism, Christianity, or Islam). The parable of the rings is the centerpiece of the drama. One ring is pure gold, and the other two are counterfeits (or are inferior quality). As the play moves along, we discover that the mind is unable to discern which is the genuine ring (the rings, of course, represent the three religions). The conclusion of the play is that the real ring has the power to lead the owner to live a compassionate life; hence ethical praxis and not metaphysical theory or theological certainty will be the path to true religion. Lessing, like Locke and Kant, moves in two directions: a theological skepticism is blended with a certain commitment to a sort of bourgeois ethical stance. This pluralist position can be found in W. C. Smith's distinctions between faith and belief. *Faith* is the realm of the personal and private religious experience and journey, and it is quite inappropriate to question or be excessively critical of such a faith stance. *Belief* is about the "accumulated traditions" within the major religious traditions; no belief system is to be given preferred status. In short, both faith and belief are to be welcomed and encouraged in the private realm. But, when the move is made to the public arena, each tradition must remember it is merely a voice in a circle of voices. There can be some common ground on ethical issues and overlap on other pressing religious questions, but it is out of place for any one tradition to assume superiority. The pluralist view, again, can be found in some forms of Indian and Buddhist thought. The parable of the many blind men—each touching various parts of an elephant and returning with a different story—speaks volumes. The Buddhist tale of the person dying with the arrow in them is about who can get the arrow out rather than who shot the arrow, what it was made of, and why it was shot. Again, we see that theological certainty is studiously avoided while a sort of ethical pragmatism wins the day. This pluralist view, then, is not new.

The pluralist model is eager and keen to support the religious quest, and it tends to do this in a non-judgmental manner. The academic study of the world's religions taps into this approach. The ideal is that religions should be studied in an empathetic and descriptive way, and evaluation, ranking, and prescription should be studiously avoided. A partisan approach to the study of religions, so it is argued, will not be objective. It should be noted that the pluralist approach is merely partisan and biased in just another way. The distinction between "fact" and "value" and the "is-ought" dilemma that has dogged much of ethics in the modern era plays into the pluralist model and its attitude toward much of the study of religion and inter-faith dialogue.

What are some of the limitations of the pluralist model? If all knowledge is finite and fallible, it can be argued that the pluralist paradigm itself is merely the product of a way of seeing and understanding the religious quest. The danger of the pluralist approach is that it sets itself up as the dominant model, and in the process excludes other forms of wisdom, knowledge, and truth claims that do not fit into its grid. It is rather ironic that many pluralists long for tolerance, but they refuse to tolerate any religions that dare to define the ban on making statements on the Ultimate. In fact, the not-so-hidden assumption of pluralism censors all sorts of issues that are basic to inter-faith dialogue. Pluralism, in short, can be most imperialistic and bully-like, and in the name of tolerance, much intolerance can rule the day. Most of the religions of the world, at their best, shy away from making final and exhaustive statements about the mystery of God, the Ultimate, the

Divine, the One. The issue is more one of which tradition has the fullest understanding of God. The pluralists are at one extreme (agnosticism) while the fundamentalists are at the other extreme (absolutists). The Christian tradition has always argued that there are important and positive things we can say and know about God (via positiva-cataphatic way), but there are also areas where it is much wiser to be silent (via negativa-apophatic way). This balanced and mystical theology is open to the general revelation of God in other cultures, but it firmly believes that "in Christ" the fullness of God was, is, and ever shall be embodied. If pluralists are truly open to allow major and minor religions to define themselves, then the ban on making final statements about the Divine (and the conflicts raised in doing so) must be lifted. When the large and challenging questions are excluded at the door, then the study of world religions and inter-faith dialogue tends to be rather tepid, tame, and artificially polite.

The pluralist model, like the exclusive and inclusive methods, excludes ways of knowing that cannot be trapped in its filter. I don't think, in the long haul, the pluralist paradigm will deepen our understanding of tolerance or inter-faith dialogue. We do not need to be tolerant if, in fact, no religious tradition (at its best) is any truer than the others. We can, of course, agree on a sort of minimal and bourgeois ethic, but there must be much more to inter-faith dialogue than this; the prophetic traditions would find this liberal pluralism good as a start but rather tame and domestic as any sort of substantive understanding of the religious vision. Pluralism, I think it can be argued, generates a sort of pseudo-tolerance, and dialogue seems a rather thin activity if, by day's end, we have learned much about other traditions but substantive evaluations are forbidden. The appeal of pluralism, of course, is its openness, but if there are no substantive criteria for determining the differences between the good, better, and best within and between traditions, we are merely trading interesting and perhaps exotic tidbits and artifacts of religious information. Pluralism must not be equated with relativism. There is a crude form of pluralism, but such a thoughtless position is not accepted by many. No serious pluralist, for example, would support the Jonestown Massacre, the Waco Texas incident, the Solar cult, and many other aberrant forms of religion. A critical pluralism, as I mentioned above, seeks a sort of common ethical ground. It also shares concerns for many other points of convergence; but, when day is done, while liberal pluralism can tell us what we should be free from (negative freedom), it tends to be weak and limp on the large and competing questions of what we are called to be free for (positive freedom).

THE SYNCRETIST MODEL

The Parliament of World's Religions has a built-in tension within it. There are those who long to welcome, without much discernment or discrimination, most of the religions of the world into a sort of cosmic parade. Each tradition is to be respected and honored, and faith communities that claim ultimacy or finality are frowned on. This form of pluralism runs against another tendency of the Parliament that speaks about a "coming unity of mankind, and a new axial age of religious oneness and universalism." Hence, there is an unresolved tension between the devotees of the Parliament about the issue of pluralism and syncretism.

The *syncretist* urge, unlike the pluralist, argues that we can know something about the final goal and end of most of the religions of the world, and the destination is, for the most part, the same. In short, there might be many paths up the mountain peak, but it is the same mountain we are all climbing, and it is the same peak we will all reach when the sun sets. Syncretism, like the inclusive model, assumes we can know what the final destination is like; pluralism is much more skeptical and reticent about such claims.

There are three forms of syncretism at the present time, and these tendencies can be found in the past as well. Syncretism, above all, places a high stress on unity, but the issue is whether unity can be achieved within time and history or if it is something that transcends time and history. The way this question is answered will determine whether one salutes at the flagpole of some version of transcendent or immanent syncretism. Those who are advocates of syncretism always are forced, out of necessity, to sacrifice decisive claims of other religions to serve their worldview. I mentioned above that the syncretist urge is not new. Emperor Alexander Severus had in his private chapel statues of Christ, Abraham, Orpheus, and deified emperors. The Muslim emperor, Akbar, attempted to form and forge a new religion in his Moghul empire that would embrace the best of other traditions. One does not have to read too far in Augustine's *Confessions* or *City of God* to get a sense of the syncretistic tendencies in the late antique Roman world. The Theosophical Society (Olcott, Blavatsky, Besant), Anthroposophy (Steiner), the American Transcendentalists (Emerson, Ellis, Channing, Brownson, Fuller), and some of the Eastern Orthodox theologians (Soloviev, Bulgakov, Berdyaev) have moved in a challenging syncretist direction with their "theosophical theology." So, syncretism, both within the history of the West and in other traditions, is nothing new. It is one way to interpret and attempt to make sense of the vast diversity of world religions; if we can say they are saying much the same thing, then many problems seem to be solved. The difficulty with such an approach, though, is that it is forced to ignore most of the facts.

The notion of immanent syncretism finds its most popular expression and organizational impetus in something like the Bahai tradition. The Bahai tradition has drawn from many of the major and minor religions of the world, and, in the process, created its own new and syncretistic religion. The Bahai tradition (founded in the nineteenth century) was not merely content to talk about the unity of religions. Bahai consciously set out to establish an organizational movement that would unite other religions. Needless to say, most of the major religions it claims to bring to the same table differ with the rather cavalier way the Bahai disciples interpret their traditions. Bahai, of course, faces the same dilemma as all syncretistic tendencies or movements. Those who do the synthesizing exclude that which does not fit into their procrustean bed. There are many within the New Age and neo-pagan movements that have syncretistic tendencies, but these particular groups are so subjective and individualistic that it is virtually impossible for them to take their highest aspirations beyond the realm of retreats, workshops, and the chosen few. The strength and advantage of Bahai, unlike New Age and neo-pagans, is the organizational issue. Bahai is committed to building a syncretistic religion for our time, and it has done a superb job of doing so; it is, without a doubt, the finest flowering of immanent syncretism in our ethos. The various types of groups in the inter-faith movement, such as the Parliament of World's Religions, The Temple of Understanding, World Congress of Faiths, Inter-Religious Federation for World Peace, and the International Association of Religious Freedom (and there are many other groups), walk the extra mile to link various faith traditions for the greater good in our global village. These groups, unlike Bahai, tend to waffle between a generous and critical pluralism and an immanent syncretism.

If Bahai and some of the inter-faith movements represent the attempt, in time, to bring many of the major and minor religions of the world around the same table; hence various forms of immanent syncretism, then the second type of syncretism is best embodied in the perennial tradition. This particular perspective is, yet once again, quite ancient, but the most modern advocates of it are Jung, Eliade, and the more popular J. Campbell. Campbell was profoundly influenced by the German cultural anthropologist, A. Bastian (1826–1905). Bastian had a great and abiding interest in myth and symbol. He was also interested in comparative mythology. Bastian made the distinction between "elementary ideas," which are universal and shared by all religions and cultures, and "ethnic or folk ideas," which are local and parochial in outlook. This turn to myth and symbol in the nineteenth century (and many others were involved) opened the floodgate for syncretism yet once again. If, in fact, when the most significant symbols and myths are unpacked and decoded, universal and elementary themes appear, then why should any religion assume it should be given preferred status? T. Carlyle, a significant Victorian author, penned his important *Sartor Resartus* with the same interest in mind; Carlyle compared varied religions to garments and clothes that people wear. We might dress and adorn ourselves in different ways from day to day, but it is the same person inside with the same anatomy. The message was clear to the alert; there are "elementary ideas" and a universal core at the center of most religions, and the various masks of the gods (Campbell) merely conceal a deeper unity. The syncretistic model can, in a more subtle and nuanced way, be found in

the quest for a theology of world religions and a universal theology of religion movement as well.

If Bahai, and to a lesser extent the inter-faith movement,
represent a type of immanent syncretism, and the *perennial
philosophy* embodies more of a mythic and transcendent syncretism, then the *Primordial tradition* is the voice and vehicle
for an esoteric syncretism. The main difference between the
perennial philosophy and the Primordial tradition is that
the former group is less committed to live from a particular tradition, whereas the Primordial tradition insists that
a person must be committed to a living tradition. The Primordial tradition was articulated, at its best, by R. Guenon,
A. Coomaraswamy, and F. Schuon. This perspective argues
that in the exoteric world of theology, myth, ritual, art, philosophy, and revelatory insight, all religions of the world are distinct and different. It is silly and pointless to try to bring them
together. In the world of time and history, the different forms
and expressions of diverse religions should be respected;
hence pluralism should dominate the day. But, it is the mystics
and contemplatives (the esoterics) who see the unity and oneness at the center and core of each religion. The esoteric realm
of the mystics, therefore, is the place of transcendent unity.
The Primordial tradition has little interest in building some
new meta-religion (like Bahai) in the world of time, but this
esoteric or mystical syncretism does argue that there is a unity
at the core of religions. The question that needs to be posed
to the Primordial tradition is this: Do, in fact, all the mystics
agree about some universal core? The answer, of course, is a
definite no.

Syncretism, then, can be seen as immanent or transcendent. Syncretism shares much with the inclusive model. Both
approaches claim to be concerned about unity, but when day

is done, the form the unity takes is decided and defined by those who articulate the vision. The various types of syncretism exclude from their perspectives those ideas that do not fit their agenda. Syntheses, as I mentioned above, always sacrifice the decisive claim of different traditions. Hence, it can be argued that the various forms of syncretism, although claiming to be tolerant and inclusive, exclude those who differ and disagree with the way they define unity and the means to reach it. The Primordial tradition elevates the esoteric mystics above the exoteric lowlanders and in the process excludes them from the deeper religious insights. The perennial tradition has, in its own way, predetermined which myths and symbols will provide guidance for the "elementary ideas" and which will be reduced to "folk and ethnic ideas"; the former group excludes the latter group from true wisdom. The Bahai tradition excludes many of the major and substantive insights of the religions they claim to include when such perspectives collide with their agenda. So, it is crucial to recognize that the exclusive tendency is at work in the inclusive, pluralist, and the syncretist models; those who would avoid this reality are not facing the hard facts.

DÉJÀ VU OR
CHRONOLOGICAL SNOBBERY?

There is a way of thinking in our midst, these days, that falsely assumes that this is a new moment in the emerging history of humanity. This fresh moment before us, in which all of the religions stand face to face, has much opportunity. Religions no more need to charge at one another, each claiming that their version of the truth is the highest and best. We are, in brief, in a new age, and this new age begs of us that we cross the Rubicon into a more creative way of understanding inter-faith relations. This unique opening in history can be compared, so the tale is told, to a Copernican revolution. Will we be like those who once thought that the earth was the center of the universe, or will we come to our senses and see that various religions, like the many planets, orbit one source of light? The choice is ours, and the arguments for crossing the Rubicon and joining the parade of the Copernican revolution are strong and compelling. Has history ever witnessed a moment like this before?

There are those, of course, with a more sophisticated knowledge of world and religious history. E. Cousins, in his challenging book, *Christ of the 21ˢᵗ Century*, argues that we are in a "second axial age." The first axial age (K. Jaspers is the source for this idea) took place between the eighth and fifth centuries BCE. This was a vibrant period of time in human history when all sorts of major and minor religions of the world appeared on the stage of human history. The first axial age saw the emergence of Taoism, Confucianism, Upanishads, Buddhism, Jainism, the Jewish prophetic tradition, classical Greek thought, and Zoroastrianism. These dispersed and compact revelations replaced the "pre-axial consciousness" that was more mythic, rooted in tribe, clan, and nature. Cousins insists that we are now in an age of "global consciousness," and this means the time has come when we must draw together and synthesize these varied and various traditions; the fate of the earth demands our urgent response. This means that our view of who Jesus the Christ was, is, and will be must take this global consciousness into consideration.

We need to ask ourselves, though, whether this enthusiasm is not a bit naive and uncritical. The "first axial age," for a starter, was not as dispersed as Cousins would like us to believe, the "pre-axial consciousness" was not quite so simplistic as Cousins makes it out to be, and the past was interested in synthesis and pluralism, inclusivism, and exclusivism. E. Voegelin, in his magisterial *The Ecumenic Age*, highlights how, from the fifth century BCE to the fifth century CE, the Roman Empire (and other empires at the time and previous to this period of time) had many a debate, discussion, and dialogue about the relationship between different religions. All sorts of major and minor religions were regularly and often in contact with one another as the empires of the time encountered and sought to conquer and colonize new territories. This, in reality, was the world, environment, and situation in which Christianity was born and matured. So, in many ways, the Christian community at the end of this century is merely back where it began.

Those like Cousins, I fear, who assume we are on the cusp of a new moment of history are, all too sadly, slipping into the typical liberal and Hegelian pitfall of chronological snobbery; the motion and movement of history will betray their highest aspirations. We have been many times in the past (in Eastern and Western civilizations) through ecumenic and inter-faith epochs. The obstinate reality of different religious traditions clearly informs us that there are, gratefully, areas of concord between religions, but the divergence and different understandings of truth and ultimate reality keep religions apart. Any serious student of religious history soon gets a nagging sense of déjà vu when the interest in pluralism and syncretism comes on the stage yet once again; will we learn nothing from our elders and the past? This drama has been seen before, and there are, no doubt, different ways of playing the parts, but the script warns us of playing fast and loose with the text. Cousins would convince us that we are in a second axial age, and it behooves us in this *kairos* moment of Teilhardian "planetization" to open ourselves to new possibilities.

There is, as I mentioned above, a sort of Hegelian religious dialectic at work in the way that Cousins is interpreting history. This Hegelian process assumes that each new epoch in history both critiques and builds on previous periods of history. This approach to history assumes that our moment in time is unique, and we have before us possibilities to forge new directions. In short, we can, if we so desire, cross the Rubicon and overcome the deficiencies of an outdated Copernican way of thinking. There is another way of reading the complex text of history, though.

It is just as valid to argue that we have been here many times before, and that the context (*agon*) of history is not about upwardness, progress, and the forward march of humanity but about many different versions of the Divine (or lack of one) competing, interpreting, and contending for truth, goodness, beauty, and justice. This approach to history means, then, a thorough reading of the drama of time and how the Christian tradition, in the present, is yet once again facing most of the same sorts of questions it has in the past. The struggle both to be self-critical (the essential role of the prophets) and to engage other religions in dialogue is not new. It is an obvious point that religious traditions do exclude one another (as do the models that are used); hence when there is a collision (as there must and will be), the task is to know how to be both charitable and faithful to a tradition. Augustine summed up such a view quite well when he stated, "*In veritate, unitas; in dubiis, libertas; in omnibus, caritas.*" Truth, when it is rightly understood, will unify us. When we are in doubt, though, and there is much room and space for uncertainty, let there be freedom and liberty. And, in all things, let the healing breeze of love and charity reign. It is wiser, therefore, to refrain from grandiose visions of global unity that will come to naught and disappoint.

It is much more insightful to realize that we have been here before many times in the unfolding drama of history, and our task is to learn from the best of the saints of the past while sidestepping many of their foolish mistakes.

ANCIENT ROOTS, NEW ROUTES

We can only move forward to the degree we are firmly grounded and rooted in the past. This is why it is essential to get back to the sources (*ad fantes*) of our ancient and time-tried tradition. The fact that we live in a multi-faith context cannot be denied. Pluralism, then, as a descriptive fact is our reality. We can take courage from the reality that the situation we live in today has many intersection points with the early church. Christianity came into being in a pluralistic and syncretistic setting, and it is crucial to note that it did not uncritically adopt either model as a way and means of being true to itself. This fact should encourage us to return to those early days and discover how the primitive, postapostolic, and patristic age (East and West) dealt with such challenging questions. We, as members of the "one, holy, catholic and apostolic church," have roots that go deep into the soil of time; these thick roots support a lush tree that has offered shade and fruit to millions throughout time (and continues to do so). This does not mean, of course, there has not been much bad fruit and many decayed branches. Pruning is an ongoing process, but the church has always recognized its need to be constantly reformed and renewed (*ecclesia semper reformanda*), and she has, also, keenly realized that though she has been justified, she continues to miss her high calling and wander astray; hence the constant and urgent need for genuine prophets.

Our task today is to realize the context we must work within and sort out how to live the good news in such a setting.

There is, of course, the much broader secular culture that either ignores religion or tinkers and dabbles with spirituality. There is a desperate need to address this audience with the depth and breadth of the Christian vision. There are, also, those who have grown up in a major or minor religious tradition (or stepped into one), and it is both the task and calling of Christians to challenge and be challenged by such traditions; this is the role of inter-faith dialogue. The models, as I mentioned above (exclusive, inclusive, pluralist, and syncretist), play an important role in how dialogue is engaged in. Each of these models has a certain appeal and limitation. I would urge us to reflect on the fact that the Christian tradition, at its wisest and best, is most at home in a prophetic exclusivism, an enlightened inclusivism, and a critical and principled pluralism. Prophetic exclusivism is the needed operative model when, on a theological or ethical level, a low view of Christ dominates the day and/or sub-human ethics sits on the throne. If, on the other hand, we encounter those (as we will) who have valid ethical insights (and live them in good faith and integrity), we should be warmly inclusive. C. S. Lewis, for example, in *The Abolition of Man* clearly highlighted the many points of convergence Christianity shares with other religious traditions when compared with the relativizing nature of much modern and post-modern thought. H. Kung, in his *Global Ethic*, has done much the same thing as Lewis. There is much that a robust Christianity can applaud and include from other religious traditions; this form of enlightened inclusivism is keen and eager to learn from other traditions. God's absolute and generous grace rains its healing waters on each and all.

The pluralist model, when seen in its proper context, should also be welcomed. Baxter once said, paraphrasing Augustine, that there should be "unity on the essentials, liberty on the non-essentials and charity in all things." There are many things in life and religion that are non-essential, and a generous pluralism should be encouraged in such a situation. Christians, it seems to me, should encourage a pluralistic political environment in which diverse religious traditions are honored and welcomed. This does not mean, though, that a sort of intellectual skepticism or a leveling of all religions should be the order of the day; a critical pluralism, grounded in certain time-tried principles, will not grant us this sort of indulgence. We should, in such a pluralistic setting, be eager to meet and greet those from other faith communities. We should also be willing to share our vision of the truth with others just as we should welcome them to unpack their vision of the truth to us. More's quote at the beginning of this article can teach us much. If pluralism merely means respect without challenge and questioning, then much vibrancy is lost and forfeited. But if challenge without respect dominates the day, evangelism becomes a form of bullying. In short, a healthy and critical pluralism creates a context within which diverse religions are honored, but dialogue and challenge also have their rightful place at the table. P. Griffiths's *An Apology for Apologetics: A Study in the Logic of Inter-Faith Dialogue* makes these telling points.

Syncretism, either of the transcendent or immanent varieties, plays on the legitimate human longing for unity, but it tends to be weak on the issue of obstinate diversity and serious differences in truth claims between religions. Most of the major and minor religious traditions of the world are quite skeptical of the rather simplistic and inconsistent claims of most syncretists. There is nothing new about the syncretistic urge, and the rocks this craft has crashed upon are always the same. The syncretist longing is valid and quite understandable, but its subtle strategy of excluding so much calls into question whether it can ever have a deep and thorough grasp of real tolerance.

We are, as I mentioned above, in a situation similar to the early Christian community. It is apt to note that the Roman Empire (like many empires and states) could be quite tolerant of different religious traditions provided these traditions remained private, personal, and kept their light under the lampstand. In short, Rome (like most states) supported some form of pluralism and syncretism. The Roman Empire walked the extra mile to support the Jewish tradition if the Jews refrained from becoming too political. The Romans, however, were not tolerant of the Jewish Zealots or messianic figures that threatened to undermine Roman national security interests. The slaughter of the innocents was not exactly a generous position of tolerance by the Romans, but it does highlight the limitations of pluralism and syncretism. Whenever Rome confronted other religious traditions (as it did quite often), it welcomed a sort of sanitized and domesticated multiculturalism that was stripped of any political, economic, social, nationalist, or ethnic content; rebellion and disagreement on these sorts of issues would not be tolerated. I fear, at times, much of the inter-faith dialogue takes place in a setting in which religion, for the most part, has been reduced to the private, personal, academic, or contemplative dimensions. This is where liberation theology and a prophetic spirituality must come to the forefront once again. If the Christian vision is going to be more than a mere personal conversion to a bourgeois ethic and lifestyle, then the prophetic voice must be heard again. There are those who, rightly so, long to return to the orthodox and classical Christian tradition; this return to the source (*ad fontes*) needs to be much more thorough and consistent, though. If we are going to be fully orthodox, in the most ecumenical sense, we must hear how the Desert Abbas-Ammas, Ambrose, Chrysostom, Becket, and many others lived. These men and women lived simply so they could give generously. These prophetic women and men challenged those in power to be true to a higher calling rather than retreat into the comfort and confines of their inner world. The kingdom of God will collide with the kingdoms of this world, and it is in such a kingdom that the costly grace of genuine evangelism and dialogue takes place.

There comes a time when we reach the end of dialogue, and it is at such moments that the church must be true to her Lord. We must walk the dialogical path as far as such a path can take us, but we need to know when we are taking a different trail to a different mountain, and such a mountain, like the Himalayas themselves, will take us to the roof of the world and beyond. The fact that the most meaningful inter-faith dialogue, in the future, will be grassroots dialogue, grounded and rooted in the human struggle for a just and meaningful world, means that our understanding of Jesus the Christ will need to be much more connected to the church and prophetic politics. If this is not done, we will restrict the light of Christ and inhibit the fullness of God's abundant grace. I began this paper with a quote from More's *Utopia*; I end with the passage at the bottom of his gravestone in St. Dunstan's parish in Canterbury. The quote reflects both the passionate thinking and life of Dunstan and More, and it points in the direction of inter-faith issues: ECCLESIA ANGLICANA LIBERA SIT.

APPENDIX

The Enlightenment, the Liberal Establishment, and Religious Pluralism

Ron Dart

The Enlightenment of the seventeenth and eighteenth centuries went in three distinct directions. The first tendency was to dismiss religion as a relic of the past; the upward and forward march of time, so it was naively thought by the secularist wing of the Enlightenment (Freud, Comte, Marx, Nietzsche, and tribe), would leave religion behind. The second direction taken was to warmly welcome religion, but no religion was to have preferred status. The humanist wing of the Enlightenment, then, unlike their secular cousins, did not attempt to ban or censor the religious impulse; they merely reduced such longings to the personal and private realms. The humanists argued that the human mind was finite and fallen, trapped in time and space; hence it is quite beyond the ken of humankind to speak with any certainty about the Ultimate, the

Divine, or God. Third, the humanists were quick to argue that many of the major and minor religions of the world shared a certain ethical code; hence there could be some important areas of consensus on ethical issues. The humanist wing of the Enlightenment, then, took a skeptical approach to the larger issue of which religious tradition is truer than the others, but there was convergence on a sort of bourgeois ethic that existed between traditions.

The liberal establishment, both within Europe and North America, tends to reflect this rather predictable Enlightenment consensus. Liberals tend to be hesitant and shy about speaking with much authority or certainty about Ultimate issues, but they can be quite firm footed when it comes to many ethical issues as they relate to a vast array of social, economic, political, cultural, and civil rights. In fact, liberals are quite keen and quick (and rightly so) to speak with conviction about various types of oppression and human rights violations within and between states. The fact that most liberals will speak with such firmness on human rights should be welcomed, but the same certainty is studiously avoided when it comes to giving the nod to one religious tradition rather than another; this reflects, of course, the Enlightenment canon and received tradition.

The CBC Massey Lectures (begun in 1961) reflect how this Enlightenment perspective, and the liberal establishment that embodies such a vision, is carried on in the Canadian context. The two major Massey Lectures that have dealt with religion have been W. C. Smith's *The Faith of Other Men* (1962) and G. Baum's *Compassion and Solidarity: The Church for Others* (1987). These lectures clearly highlight my point. Smith makes the important distinction between faith and belief. *Faith* is personal, and each and all should respect and honor another's faith journey. *Belief* is about the "accumulated traditions" within faith communities, and Smith, predictably, does not evaluate which tradition is truer or more valid than others. Baum, of course, spends all of his lectures on the importance of compassion and solidarity as basic to the vision of the church; in short, Christianity, if it is going to be given a voice within the liberal establishment, must concern itself with ethics, but more to the point it must reflect the ethics of social liberalism. Baum does this well; hence he is chosen to give the lectures. Most of the Massey Lectures reflect a sort of broad social liberalism that the liberal establishment eagerly and uncritically genuflects before. The tolerance of social liberalism is, usually, confined to those who remain agnostic about which religious tradition is better than others and those who salute at their flagpole in the culture wars. Social liberalism, then, is a worldview that includes a perspective and excludes much as well.

Our modern ethos of multiculturalism (and religious pluralism), therefore, is framed within the context of both the humanistic Enlightenment tradition and the liberal establishment (who are the guardians and gatekeepers). Those who hope and long to be accepted, recognized, and promoted within this tradition must, predictably, be rather neutral or silent on the question of the superiority of one religious tradition in comparison to others; such a social liberalism must also have a certain restrained conscience for ethical issues; those who are either too radical on the left or too far to the corporate and business right will be marginalized from the dialogue. Religious pluralism, then, is the dominant tradition of the liberal establishment. This means that any religious tradition that dares to break the ban on religious neutrality will be, quite predictably, marginalized by the mandarins of the hegemonic culture. There is no doubt that religious pluralism exists as a legitimate check against the aberrations of the religious impulse that can go amuck, but those who dare to think from a position of critical theory (rather than merely saluting at the shrine of Enlightenment social liberalism) need to raise some troubling and nagging doubts about the validity of religious pluralism itself. How and should the spell be broken? Is it possible to engage in the difficult questions of good, better, best and bad, worse, worst without slipping into reactionary fundamentalism? It certainly is, and a much deeper religious pluralism might take us in this direction. Perhaps this is the path of a prophetic exclusivism and an enlightened inclusivism.

RECOMMENDED READING

Barrett, Clive. *To the Fathers They Shall Go: Wealth and Poverty in Early Christian Thought.* London: Jubilee Group, 1984.

Berrigan, Daniel, and Thich Nhat Hanh. *The Raft Is Not the Shore: Conversations Toward a Buddhist-Christian Awareness.* Maryknoll, NY: Orbis, 1975.

Copleston, Frederick C. *Religion and the One: Philosophies East and West.* New York: Crossroad, 1982.

D'arcy, Martin. *The Meeting of Love and Knowledge: Perennial Wisdom.* New York: Harper, 1957.

Griffiths, Bede. *The Marriage of West and East.* Springfield, IL: Templegate, 1982.

Leech, Kenneth. *Subversive Orthodoxy: Traditional Faith and Radical Orthodoxy.* Toronto: Anglican Book Centre, 1992.

Merton, Thomas. *Zen and the Birds of Appetite.* New York: New Directions, 1968.

———. *Mystics and Zen Masters.* New York: Delta, 1961.

Panikkar, Raimon. *The Intra-Religious Dialogue.* New York: Paulist Press, 1970.

Parrinder, Geoffrey. *Mysticism in the World's Religions.* London: Sheldon Press, 1976.

———. *Avatar and Incarnation.* London: Faber & Faber, 1970.

———. *Jesus in the Qu'rān.* New York: Barnes and Noble, 1955.

———. *Upanishads, Gita and Bible.* London: Sheldon Press, 1975.

Reckitt, Maurice B. *For Christ and the People: Studies of Four Socialist Priests and Prophets of the Church of England Between 1870 and 1930.* London: SPCK, 1968.

Sharpe, Eric J. *Faith Meets Faith: Some Christian Attitudes to Hinduism in the Nineteenth and Twentieth Centuries.* London: SCM Press, 1977.

———. *Comparative Religion: A History.* Richmond, VA: Knox, 1971.

Zaehner, Robert Charles. *Mysticism: Sacred and Profane: An Inquiry into Some Varieties of Praeternatural Experience.* London: Oxford University Press, 1961.

———. *Concordant Discord: The Interdependence of Faiths.* Oxford: The Clarendon Press, 1970.